DATE DUE 6/20

			PRINTED IN U.S.A.

12 ARCHITECTS
WHO CHANGED THE WORLD

by Vicki C. Hayes

12

STORY LIBRARY

MORE TO EXPLORE

www.12StoryLibrary.com

12-Story Library is an imprint of Bookstaves.

Photographs ©: Nick Moore/Alamy, cover, 1; Dmitry Ternovoy/FAL, 4; Steven Liveoak/Shutterstock.com, 5; sefer/CC3.0, 5; PD, 6; Sean Pavone/Shutterstock.com, 7; mark reinstein/Shutterstock.com, 8; Bumble Dee/Shutterstock.com, 9; Jer123/Shutterstock.com, 9; Jonathan Brady/Alamy, 10; serhatk/Shutterstock.com, 11; CC4.0, 12; King of Hearts/CC3.0, 13; Hans van Dijk/Anefo/CC3.0, 14; f11photo/Shutterstock.com, 15; elfarero/Shutterstock.com, 15; blackpast.org/PD, 16; Rs1421/CC3.0, 17; Pau Audouard Deglaire/PD, 18; Baldomer Gili i Roig/PD, 19; Mapics/Shutterstock.com, 19; Ringo Chiu/Alamy, 20; clayton harrison/Shutterstock.com, 21; FEMA/Kenneth Wilsey/PD, 21; Keystone Press/Alamy, 22; Alexandre Norman/CC3.0, 23; Lynn Gilbert/CC4.0, 24; WhisperToMe/PD, 25; Michael Dwyer/Associated Press, 26; CC3.0, 27; meunierd/Shutterstock.com, 27; Neri Oxman/CC4.0, 28; Radomir Rezny/Shutterstock.com, 29

ISBN
9781632357120 (hardcover)
9781632358219 (paperback)
9781645820000 (ebook)

Library of Congress Control Number: 2019938615

Printed in the United States of America
July 2019

About the Cover
Zaha Hadid in 2011.

Access free, up-to-date content on this topic plus a full digital version of this book. Scan the QR code on page 31 or use your school's login at 12StoryLibrary.com.

Table of Contents

Zaha Hadid: Pushing the Limits

Zaha Hadid was an architect, designer, and teacher. She was born in Baghdad, Iraq, in 1950. She went to college in Lebanon. Then she moved to London to study architecture.

Hadid enjoyed designing buildings. She designed museums, opera houses, parking garages, and even ski jumps. Her designs were geometric. Her buildings looked like they were moving. She designed a fire station in Germany that looked like a flying bird. She designed a swimming center in London that looked like moving water.

Hadid experimented with design. She sometimes pushed the limits of architecture. Some of her designs were never built. They were thought to be too unusual. Instead, many of her drawings were put in art museums. For this reason, she was sometimes called a "paper architect."

Hadid also designed furniture, jewelry, shoes, and lighting. In 2014, she designed a stage set for *Cosi fan tutte*, an opera by Mozart.

Hadid taught architecture at several large universities. She won many awards for her buildings and for her furniture. Hadid died in 2016 at age 65.

Zaha Hadid in 2013.

Heydar Aliyev Cultural Center in Baku, Azerbaijan.

THE PRITZKER ARCHITECTURE PRIZE

The Pritzker Prize is an international prize for architects. It is the highest honor a living architect can earn. To win, architects must do several things. They must show a lot of talent. They must design a lot of buildings, and their building designs must help people. The winner gets $100,000. In 2004, Zaha Hadid was the first woman ever to win this important prize.

100
Awards and honors Zaha Hadid won in her lifetime

- The Stirling Prize is the highest architecture award in the United Kingdom.
- Hadid won the Stirling Prize twice.
- In 2012, she was made a Dame of the British Empire.

Frank Lloyd Wright: Greatest American Architect

Frank Lloyd Wright was born in 1867 in Wisconsin. He got his love of form and design from his mother.

Wright started his design work in Chicago after college. His work was considered beautiful because it was simple. He liked natural beauty instead of fancy designs. Many of his projects were private homes. He was very good at making a house fit the land around it. He designed a house in Pennsylvania called Fallingwater. It was built over a waterfall.

Wright invented two types of house design. They were called Prairie Style and Usonian. Prairie Style houses were long and low and built using local materials. Usonian houses were simple and not too expensive. They had several new features.

Wright's Imperial Hotel was demolished in 1967, but the entrance courtyard and pool were rebuilt in an open-air museum in Nagoya, Japan.

IMPERIAL HOTEL, TOKYO, JAPAN

532

Number of designs by Frank Lloyd Wright that were actually built

- Wright designed 1,114 projects overall.
- He wanted everything in his buildings to go together.
- He designed the furniture, the rugs, the lights, and even the dishes.

THINK ABOUT IT

As a child, Wright played with blocks. He said the blocks influenced his later designs. Think about the toys you play with. How might they influence your choice of career?

These included solar heating, natural cooling, and carports.

Wright also designed larger buildings. He designed the Imperial Hotel in Tokyo. He said it was earthquake-proof. One year later, it was the only large building left standing after an earthquake hit the city. Wright designed a museum in New York City called the Guggenheim. It is a large white building shaped like a spiraling cylinder. There is one long walkway that coils up from the ground floor. Visitors take an elevator to the top. Then they walk down the ramp and look at the art.

Frank Lloyd Wright designed buildings for seven decades. He is thought of as the greatest American architect.

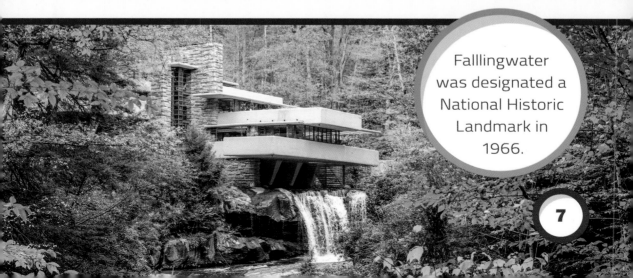

Falllingwater was designated a National Historic Landmark in 1966.

Maya Lin: Fitting into Nature

Maya Lin is a Chinese American architect. Her parents fled China as the Communists were taking over. Maya was born in Athens, Ohio, in 1959. As a child, she loved animals, nature, and walks in the woods. These loves influenced her later designs.

When she was only 21 and still in college, Lin won a design contest. The contest was for the Vietnam Veterans Memorial in Washington, DC. The memorial is two granite walls that slowly rise from the ground and meet, like sides of a triangle. Each wall is 246 feet 9 inches long (about 75 m). Carved on the walls are thousands of names. They are all United States service members who died because of the Vietnam War (1954–1975).

Lin likes her work to fit into the environment. She wants it to look like it belongs in nature. Sometimes it can be hard to find her work, it blends in so well. She designed a sculpture at the University of Michigan. It was undulating soil covered in grass. She designed a memorial in Alabama. It was a black stone beneath a thin layer of moving water. She

In 1981, Lin demonstrated the angles of the walls for the Vietnam Veterans Memorial.

designed a park at Ohio University. It is best seen from the air. It looks like an old-fashioned computer punch card. Lin's indoor sculptures are also all about the environment.

The names on the wall are listed by date of casualty from the beginning of the war until the end.

58,318
Names engraved on the granite wall of the Vietnam Veterans Memorial

- At first, many people said Lin's design was ugly and even shameful.
- Today, this is the most visited monument in Washington, DC.
- More than 10,000 people visit the Vietnam Veterans Memorial each day.

THINK ABOUT IT

When some people learned Maya Lin was young, female, and Chinese American, they thought the design for the Vietnam Memorial should be changed. Why do you think this was?

David Adjaye: Visionary Architect

David Adjaye was born in Tanzania in 1966 to parents from Ghana. He spent his childhood living in Africa and the Middle East. He saw many different cultures and their unique building styles. As a teenager, he moved with his family to England.

After graduating from college, Adjaye formed his own architecture company. His first designs were for stores, restaurants, and houses. Then he worked on larger public buildings. These included a museum, a school, and a peace center. His buildings are all very different. They are designed to reflect the space around them.

Many people thought Adjaye was too young to work on such big projects. But Adjaye persisted. In 2009, he was chosen for an important project.

It was a new Smithsonian museum in Washington, DC. It was called the National Museum of African American History and Culture (NMAAHC). Adjaye's winning design was influenced by two factors in his life. One was the traveling he did as a child. Because he visited so many countries, he learned to be sensitive to different cultures. The other factor was his younger brother, who always used a wheelchair. Adjaye knew from personal experience that buildings

Sir David Adjaye, after he was knighted in 2017.

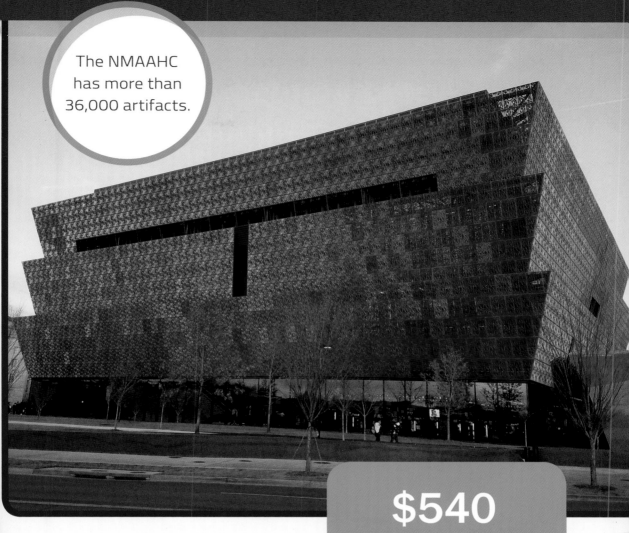

The NMAAHC has more than 36,000 artifacts.

had to be sensitive to people's needs.

Adjaye has won many architecture awards. He has even been knighted by the British Empire. He is also a photographer. On his travels to each capital city in every African country, he took photos. His photographs have been published in seven large volumes.

$540 million
Cost to build the NMAAHC

- The museum opened in Washington, DC, in 2016.
- It is the 19th Smithsonian museum.
- The exterior design reflects West African sculpture and New Orleans ironwork.

Julia Morgan: Pioneering Female Architect

Julia Morgan circa 1900.

first woman to graduate from the school.

In 1904, Morgan returned to San Francisco. She opened her own architecture firm. Then came the San Francisco earthquake of 1906. Hundreds of buildings were destroyed. This was an opportunity for Morgan. She designed more than 700 homes, churches, offices, stores, and schools.

Julia Morgan was born to a wealthy San Francisco family in 1872. She got a degree in engineering. Then she decided to study architecture. She wanted to attend an art school in Paris called l'Ecole des Beaux-arts. The school wouldn't admit her because she was a woman. Two years later, she was admitted. She became the

80
Percentage of buildings in San Francisco destroyed by the 1906 earthquake

- Three years earlier, Morgan had designed a bell tower at Mills College in nearby Oakland.
- It was still standing after the earthquake.
- Because of this, she was hired to design the grand Fairmont Hotel.

Morgan was known for her outstanding designs and craftsmanship. One of her most famous buildings was Hearst Castle. It was designed for a wealthy newspaper publisher.

Morgan was the first woman to be a professional architect in California. She was one of the most important woman architects in the United States. She designed buildings for over four decades. In 2014, 57 years after her death, she was awarded a Gold Medal from the American Institute of Architects. This is the AIA's highest honor. Morgan was the first woman to receive this award.

The Hearst Castle was built between 1919 and 1947.

HEARST CASTLE

William Randolph Hearst was a very rich man. He owned 250,000 acres of land in California. He hired Julia Morgan to design buildings for a retreat there. Hearst Castle is the main building. It has 115 rooms, including 38 bedrooms and 42 bathrooms. There are also three guesthouses. The grounds have pools and waterfalls. There was even a zoo at one time.

Kenzo Tange: Designing for the Human Heart

Kenzo Tange in 1981.

inspired. He went on to become Japan's most famous architect.

Tange was very interested in city planning. One city he planned was Hiroshima. This Japanese city was destroyed in World War II by the first atomic bomb. Tange planned the new city. He also designed the Hiroshima Peace Memorial Park. He wanted to show the human longing for peace. The city was built around the park. Tange went on to design other cities damaged by war.

Tange also designed offices, churches, and two gyms for the Tokyo Olympics. In 1960, he designed ways to make the city of Tokyo bigger. His ideas included building bridges, islands, and floating parking. Most of his designs were for buildings in Japan. But he also designed buildings in other countries.

Kenzo Tange was born in Japan in 1913. He never thought of becoming an architect. Then, in college, he studied the work of Le Corbusier, the Swiss-French architect. Tange was

Tange won the Pritzker Architecture Prize in 1987. He also won Japan's highest prize for architecture.

The Hiroshima Peace Memorial has a Peace Flame that has burned continuously since it was lit in 1964.

CHILDREN'S PEACE MONUMENT

Sasaki Sadako lived in Hiroshima. Radiation from the bomb gave her cancer. She hoped that folding paper cranes would keep her alive. She folded 1,300, but she died at the age of 12. Her classmates designed a monument to her. It was also to all children who died because of the bomb. People who visit the monument bring paper cranes. Today there are over 10 million cranes at the monument.

1950

Year when Tange designed the Hiroshima Peace Memorial Park

- The park has a Peace Center, a museum, and a Children's Peace Monument.
- The Peace Center combines traditional and modern Japanese architecture styles.
- Tange included many trees in the park as grave markers for the dead.

7

Norma Sklarek: The Rosa Parks of Architecture

Norma Sklarek circa 1978.

took the architecture licensing examination and passed it on her first try. She became the first black woman with an architect license in New York State. She got hired by a firm. But she was given lowly jobs like designing bathrooms.

In 1960, Sklarek moved to Los Angeles and took another licensing exam. She became the first black woman to get an architect license in California. She got a job at a big firm and designed many projects. But she was always called the project manager. The company did not want their clients to know a black woman had designed their projects. In 1966, she became director of the firm.

In 1985, Sklarek started her own firm. It only used women architects. It was the largest woman-owned architecture firm in the United States. After a few years, she

Norma Sklarek was born in New York City in 1926. She went to Barnard College, then Columbia University, where she majored in architecture. She was the first black woman to get a degree in architecture. Then she went looking for a job. Nineteen firms turned her down. They were not hiring blacks or women. In 1954, Sklarek

10,000

Number of African American architects today

- Sklarek coached young architects who wanted to take the licensing exam.
- Howard University has a scholarship in Sklarek's name.
- In 1980, she became a fellow at the American Institute of Architects.

left to work at a bigger company. She continued her work for many decades. She designed the original Terminal One at the Los Angeles International Airport. She designed the United States Embassy in Tokyo. She also worked on the Mall of America in Minneapolis.

Sklarek broke barriers. She became a role model for others. Because of this, she is sometimes called the Rosa Parks of Architecture.

The US Embassy in Tokyo was completed in 1976.

Antoni Gaudi: One of a Kind

Antoni Gaudi in 1878.

Antoni Gaudi was born in Spain in 1852. His father was a coppersmith, but not Gaudi. From an early age, he was interested in nature and in architecture. At 16, he went to Barcelona to study architecture. Most of his best works are in that city.

Gaudi's works were often inspired by nature. He did not like to use straight lines or angles. He said they didn't occur in nature. Instead, he used curves and shapes such as parabolic and hyperbolic forms. He often covered the surfaces of these shapes with colorful decorations. He used patterned brick, stone, or bright ceramics. He used green and white checkerboard patterns and floral tiles.

Gaudi's works were often described as vibrant and flamboyant. He used pointed arches, balconies that stuck out, and rooftop turrets. He designed iron grilles that looked like vines or tangled seaweed. He loved spires and put 18 of them on one of his buildings.

In 1883, he designed his most famous building. It was a cathedral in Barcelona called Sagrada Familia. In 1915, he stopped all his other work and focused only on this project. He worked on it until his death 11 years later. Gaudi is Spain's most famous architect. Seven of his sites are World Heritage Sites.

Construction in 1905.

The Sagrada Familia in 2016.

135+
Years spent to date on the construction of Sagrada Familia

- The cathedral has four spires.
- It is scheduled to be completed in 2026.
- At that point, it will be the tallest church in Europe.

WORLD HERITAGE SITES

UNESCO wanted to find and save outstanding cultural sites in the world. They set up a committee to choose these sites. To be selected, a site or building had to show human creative genius. It had to have special importance and be unique in one of several ways. Today there are over 1,000 sites worldwide.

Mia Lehrer: Landscape Architect

32
Miles of river that pass through Los Angeles

- The Master Plan has 240 different projects.
- These projects will affect thousands of streets and neighborhoods.
- The plan will connect communities and change the way people think of the river.

Mia Lehrer was born in 1952 in El Salvador. She grew up exploring beaches, forests, and volcanoes. Her parents taught her to respect the land and care for the earth. She came to the United States to attend college. She saw a program about Frederick Law Olmsted. He was the designer of Central Park in New York City. Lehrer decided to become a landscape architect.

Lehrer works to make cities look and feel better. She makes streets and neighborhoods more attractive. She makes beautiful riversides and large urban parks. She thinks landscape designers should make cities more livable. They should make spaces for recreation and reflection. She has designed beach houses, waterfronts, parks, and outdoor gardens.

Lehrer's biggest project is a design for the Los Angeles River. This waterway runs through downtown Los Angeles. It is lined with concrete. In 2007, Lehrer was lead

Bike paths exist along parts of the Los Angeles River today.

CENTRAL PARK

Central Park is a 750-acre park in midtown Manhattan. It was designed by Frederick Law Olmsted 160 years ago. Central Park provides peace and tranquility in the midst of one of the largest cities in the United States. It has woodlands, streams, and walkways. There are places for music, boating, ice skating, baseball, and more. Today the park is a vital part of New York City.

author on the Los Angeles River Master Plan. The plan will restore public space along the river. Lehrer believes that nature must exist in cities. In 2007, she became a fellow in the American Society of Landscape Architects.

Le Corbusier: Designing for Modern Times

Le Corbusier in 1962.

to make better housing for people in large cities. His building designs were simple and geometric. They had pillars, roof terraces, open floor plans, and very little decoration. He was one of the first architects to use lots of concrete. However, not everyone liked his ideas. In Pessac, France, he built a workers' city of 40 houses. The local government would not connect them to the public water supply. They said the buildings were too colorful and unusual.

Le Corbusier was born in the mountains of Switzerland in 1887. As a teenager, he joined his father as a watch engraver. Then he took a trip through Europe. He became interested in buildings and structure. He taught himself to be an architect.

Le Corbusier's first years were spent on city planning. He wanted

After World War II, Le Corbusier designed his first large housing project. It was in Marseille, France. He also designed apartment buildings and private homes. He even designed a home in Switzerland for his parents. In 2016, 17 of his buildings in 7 different countries were named World Heritage Sites.

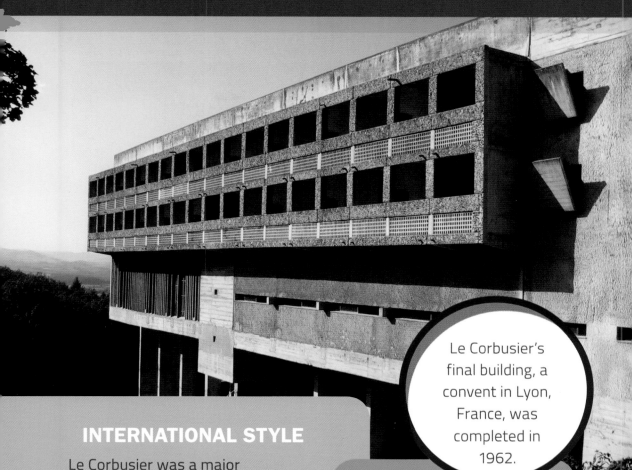

Le Corbusier's final building, a convent in Lyon, France, was completed in 1962.

INTERNATIONAL STYLE

Le Corbusier was a major contributor to a design movement called the International Style. This was considered a modern style for modern times. It used clean lines and emphasized sleek efficiency. The most common building materials were steel, glass, and reinforced concrete. The internal structure of the building was often exposed. Decorative features were considered old-fashioned. Today's skyscrapers are often built in the International Style.

1,800
Number of residents in Le Corbusier's Marseille housing project

- The building was meant to be a community.
- It had 18 floors and 23 types of split-level apartments.
- It also had shops, a school, a hotel, a gym, and a theater.

Denise Scott Brown: More than a Wife

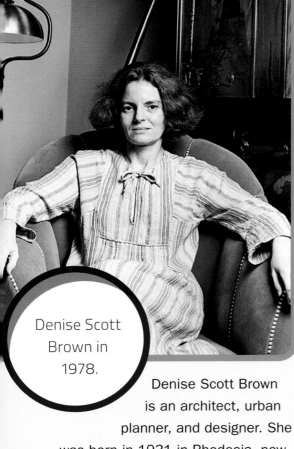

Denise Scott Brown in 1978.

Denise Scott Brown is an architect, urban planner, and designer. She was born in 1931 in Rhodesia, now Zambia. She studied architecture in London. Then she came to the United States. She met Robert Venturi while teaching at the University of Pennsylvania.

He was also an architect. They were soon married.

Scott Brown's focus was on urban planning. She helped small towns save their old buildings and preserve their heritage. But most of her work was done with her husband. She and Venturi designed homes, museums, and furniture. They worked together on an important book called *Learning from Las Vegas*. They looked at the architecture of the city. They looked at the cars, the signs, and other cultural symbols. They said these things were important in architecture.

In 1991, Scott Brown's husband won the Pritzker Prize for his work. Venturi insisted that all the work had been done jointly. But the committee would not recognize Scott Brown. She decided not to attend the award ceremony. She wrote an essay. She described how hard it had been for her to be seen as an equal partner in the architecture world. She spoke out for women in architecture. She still speaks about discrimination within the profession.

THINK ABOUT IT

The Pritzker Committee rejected the petition because they said their award could only be given to one person. They could not change the rules. What do you think about that?

20,000+

Signatures on a petition asking the Pritzker Committee to recognize Denise Scott Brown

- In 2013, the petition was rejected.
- In 2016, Scott Brown and Venturi jointly won the AIA Gold Medal.
- In 2017, Scott Brown won the Jane Drew Prize for women in architecture.

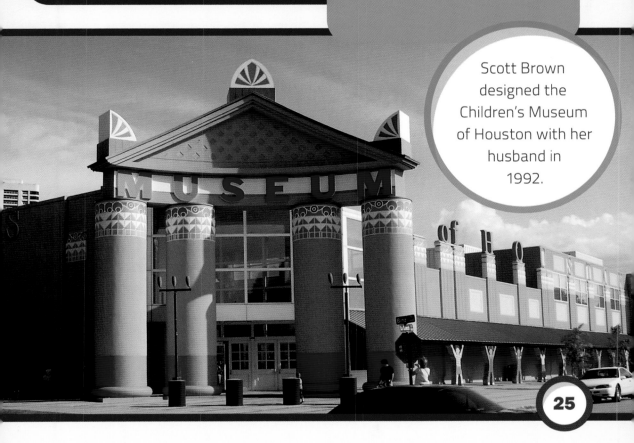

Scott Brown designed the Children's Museum of Houston with her husband in 1992.

Moshe Safdie: Design with Meaning

Safdie in 2003.

Moshe Safdie is an Israeli-Canadian-American architect and urban designer. He was born in Israel in 1938. He attended college in Canada. Currently, he heads his own firm in Boston.

Safdie's most famous building was built in 1967 for the Montreal World's Fair. It was a housing complex called Habitat '67. The apartments were boxes made of prefabricated concrete. They were stacked in uneven patterns. Every apartment had a garden or terrace. In the 1970s, Safdie worked to rebuild the city of Jerusalem. In Canada, he designed six important public institutions including Vancouver Library Square.

Safdie believes buildings should have meaningful spaces. They should add to the local geography and culture. There should be a connection between beauty and purpose. Buildings need to create spaces that bring the community together.

Over his 50-year career, Safdie has designed projects all over the world. These include airports, museums, libraries, houses, and even entire cities. His designs have dramatic curves and complex geometric patterns. They have lots of open, green spaces and many windows.

2,560
Hotel rooms in Moshe Safdie's Marina Bay Sands hotel in Singapore

- The complex has three 55-story towers connected on top by a 3-acre (1.2 hectare) garden.
- There is an infinity swimming pool 500 feet (150 m) high.
- A fourth tower, with 1,000 suites, is planned for the near future.

The Marina Bay Sands hotel.

One recent project is the Crystal Bridges Museum of American Art in Arkansas. Several pavilions are set into a large natural ravine. They are surrounded by ponds, bridges, gardens, and hiking trails. Another is Changi Airport in Singapore. It houses an indoor forest with gardens and walking trails. The glass domed roof is 130 feet high (40 m). Pouring down from the center is the world's tallest indoor waterfall.

Over 50 years after they were built, Safdie's Habitat '67 consists of 148 apartments today.

More Architects Who Changed the World

Jeanne Gang

Jeanne Gang (1964-) is an American architect born in Illinois. She designs homes, schools, and office buildings. Her buildings have been called poetry for the eyes. She is best known for the 2010 design of a Chicago skyscraper called Aqua Tower. From a distance, the 82-story building looks like a wavy sculpture. Up close, the waves are actually windows and porches. Gang also works to make her buildings energy efficient.

Neri Oxman

Neri Oxman (1976-) is an Israeli-American architect. She is known for creating "material ecology." She uses computer design, synthetic biology, and 3-D printing to make objects. She uses natural organisms such as mushrooms, moss, slime mold, and monarch butterflies. One of her most famous structures is the Silk Pavilion. First, a nylon-framed dome was loosely woven by a robot arm. Then the surface was completed by 6,500 free-ranging silkworms.

Silkworms made Oxman's Silk Pavillion structure.

The Aqua Tower in Chicago.

I.M. Pei

I.M. Pei (1917–2019) was a Chinese-American architect. He designed important projects all over the world. His buildings are large and elegant. His architecture combines circles, squares, and triangles. Some of his well-known buildings include the Holocaust Museum in Washington, DC, and the Rock and Roll Hall of Fame in Cleveland, Ohio. Perhaps his best-known structure is the glass pyramid in front of the Louvre Museum in Paris.

Christopher Wren

Christopher Wren (1632–1723) was the greatest English architect of his time. His first design was for a theater. Then, in 1666, the Great Fire of London destroyed two-thirds of the city. This was devastating to London, but it gave Wren an opportunity. He rebuilt 52 churches, including his most famous, St. Paul's Cathedral. St. Paul's took 53 years to finish. Wren also designed a royal observatory and several royal palaces.

Glossary

discrimination
The unfair treatment of people based on factors like race, gender, or age.

duplex
A house with two separate apartments.

flamboyant
Very elaborate or fancy.

heritage
Qualities or objects or buildings passed down from generation to generation.

hyperbolic
A shape with two parabolic curves that mirror each other.

parabolic
A curve that resembles the arc an object makes when you kick it up in the air.

pavilion
A building used in a park or large garden.

prefabricated
Made ahead of time in sections for easy assembly.

preservation
Keeping something in its original state.

reinforced
Strengthened with additional support.

undulating
Rising and falling.

Read More

Alphin, Tom. *The LEGO Architect.* San Francisco, CA: No Starch Press, 2015.

Armstrong, Simon. *Cool Architecture: Filled with Fantastic Facts for Kids of All Ages.* London, UK: Pavilion, 2015.

Beck, Barbara. *The Future Architect's Tool Kit.* Atglen, PA: Schiffer Publishing, 2016.

Rubin, Susan Goldman. *Maya Lin: Thinking with Her Hands.* San Francisco, CA: Chronicle Books, 2017.

Teegarden, Catherine. *How to Think Like Frank Lloyd Wright: Creative Activities to Inspire.* New York: Downtown Bookworks, 2019.

Visit 12StoryLibrary.com

Scan the code or use your school's login at **12StoryLibrary.com** for recent updates about this topic and a full digital version of this book. Enjoy free access to:

- Digital ebook
- Breaking news updates
- Live content feeds
- Videos, interactive maps, and graphics
- Additional web resources

Note to educators: Visit 12StoryLibrary.com/register to sign up for free premium website access. Enjoy live content plus a full digital version of every 12-Story Library book you own for every student at your school.

Index

About the Author

Vicki C. Hayes currently works as a
teacher and writer. She loved doing
the research for this book and now
has a list of amazing buildings to visit.

READ MORE FROM 12-STORY LIBRARY

Every 12-Story Library Book
is available in many fomats.
For more information, visit
12StoryLibrary.com